I Used to be a Superwoman

By
Gloria Velásquez

Arte Público Press
Houston, Texas

This volume is made possible through grants from the
National Endowment for the Arts (a federal agency), Andrew W. Mellon
Foundation, the Lila Wallace-Reader's Digest Fund and the City of Houston
through theCultural Arts Council of Houston, Harris County.

Recovering the past, creating the future

Arte Público Press
University of Houston
Houston, Texas 77204-2090

Cover design by Susan Barber
Original art by G. Bermúdez
Book design by Debora Fisher

I Used to be a Superwoman

By
Gloria Velásquez

Acknowledgments

The publication of this book represents the fulfillment of a dream that began when I was a little girl living on the patrón's ranches. There have been many people along the way who have provided me with the strength and courage to complete this dream. I wish to thank my parents, Juan y Francisca Velásquez, for giving me that lust for life despite their economic hardships. I am deeply indebted to Carlos Leal, Arsenio Sandoval, Ray Romero and George Keating for inspiring me and being my role-models. I also wish to thank Francisco Alarcón, Patricia Montenegro, Manuel Hernández, Kathleen Newman, and our beloved Arturo Islas, for encouraging me to keep writing. And without the love and support of mis hijitos, Bobby and Brandi, and my inspirational comadre, Kay Magill, nothing would be possible. Lastly, much love and gratitude to G. Bermúdez for the beautiful cover art and a special thanks to my editors, Yolanda and Ernesto Padilla for believing in this manuscript, to my friend, Guillermo Little for helping me smooth out the translations and Margarita Luna Robles for her kind words.

I wish to thank the following journals and anthologies where some of the poems in this collection first appeared: *El Tecolote Literario, Aurora, Caracol, Metamorfosis, La voz de Colorado, From the Midwest to the West, Canto al pueblo: Anthology of Experiences, Grito del sol, La Luz, El diario de la gente, Maíze, Mestizo, Bilingual Review, Recent Chicano Poetry: Neueste Chicano Lyrik, Children of La Frontera* and *Sendas literarias*.

Contents

I Used to be a Superwoman: The Polemics of a Chicana's Poetic Voice

The poet's eye, in a fine frenzy rolling,
Doth glance from heaven to earth, from earth to heaven;
And as imagination bodies forth
The forms of things unknown, the poet's pen
Turns them to shapes, and gives to airy nothing
A local habitation and a name.

William Shakespeare

As long as I've been a poet I have been plagued with the challenge of, "Is this a poem, or, what makes this thing I've written a poem?" this question is rooted in the center of my being: Chicana. The question comes with the territory, the colloquialism becoming literal and not metaphorical. That is—because I live in the United States and I write poetry but my ancestry comes from Mexico—this automatically implies that perhaps my work as an artist is not as good as...and the assumption will be made that everything I write will be political. This of course leads to the polemic of political poetry not being "good" poetry, or the basic argument of esthetics, of low and high art. Who holds the measuring stick? Gloria Velásquez, like me, is plagued by this polemic.

I Used to be a Superwoman is a collection of poems that reads like diary entries in the life of a Chicana. Gloria takes us through phases of her life and shares with us the moment. Denise Levertov in *Light Up the Cave* has said that a "poet is only a poet when engaged in making poems, and has no rightful claim to *feeling* more than others, but only to being able to *articulate* feeling through the medium of language." In every poem, Gloria arrives at the *feeling* and the reader becomes engaged. The simplicity of her language makes the experience accessible.

The first poem, "Poverty" immediately takes us to Gloria's Childhood. The poem resonates, for most Chicanos, our own childhood. In American pop culture, most Baby Boomers relate to the *Happy Days* mentality of the fifties as evident in television shows such as *Leave It To Beaver, The Donna Reed Show, Father Knows Best* and *The Ozzie and Harriet Show*. Not us Brownies—we did not have Donna or Harriet in a frilly apron waiting for us with cookies and milk in a suburban maze home when we came home from school. What was home like for us? A two-room shack with a communal bathroom somewhere outside; an aluminum tub with cold water poured in from the nearest faucet; a petroleum stove warming beans and tortillas. Mamá y Papá would arrive at sundown, beaten from the sun's heat and toil of the earth, beaten by the elements our ancestors had once worshipped:

> Poverty devours all that is beautiful
> leaving behind that
> which is called hunger—
> hunger for survival.

In "Memories," "Wonderful Youth" and "Children of the Sun" the childhood journeys evolve. The travels do not relate what children might write in a school assignment about what they did during the summer. The journeys are the migrant fieldworker maps followed by many Mexicanos from the late 19th century to the present. Yes, the migrant farmworker trails exist:

> I learned about summer vacations,
> swimming pools and suntans,
> stooped down in the beetfields
> with a hoe in my hand
> suffering the sun's heat ("Wonderful Youth")

"Thou Art" is a political poem—and a good one. It is a poem for the American Flag, symbol of our country, America:

> But I remember the coffin
> of a young soldier
> who was once covered with your bright colors.
> ...But I remember the tears
> that my mother cried
> as she held you tight
> and the bullets rang out.
> You're so beautiful!"

Throughout this collection, Gloria remembers her brother, Fini, who died in Viet Nam. Fini appears in the poems in almost a haunting manner, but what is driving in these poetic texts is a Chicana consciousness. Viet Nam was a useless war and there were more Chicanos killed in Viet Nam (grossly disproportionate numbers by percentage) than any other ethnic group. Many Chicanos went to Viet Nam to escape the barrio, unemployment, lack of access to education, prison, the fields. In "From *Good Morning Vietnam* to Good Morning, Mamá" Gloria asks, "Did you remember him today, mom, that child you carried in your womb those winter days when you didn't even know where the next day's meal was coming from, those days of poverty, of borrowed houses, cold-hearted *patrones* and a small cold room where the son you adored was born?" The irony of Vietnam for us Chicanos is the outcome: a Chicano's tour of duty did not change reality. Most Chicanos who made it back returned to what they had tried to escape, the barrio, unemployment, lack of access to education, prison, the fields.

Gloria's poems are driven by her womaness. The sensibilities in her text and themes—as simple as they might seem because of the simplicity of language—are heartfelt and complex. What seems to be a light brush stroke of an image becomes a finely executed wave in a landscape called *mujer.* Gloria offers flowers, incense and old *cantos.* These poems sing and breathe the essence of her being. She takes us to her childhood, to her mother's side and shows us the vulnerability of being Chicana, acknowledging her Navajo past. She puts the childhood fears away and takes us to Stanford to witness her metamorphosis. We are born with her and can't help but feel the rejoicing—she won't ever have to go back to that painful past. In "Realism" we see that contrast:

> Over there,
> > my drunken father
> > > my mother with swollen feet
> > > my grandfather haunting the streets,
>
> And me here,
> > imprisoned at Stanford
> > > far away from my *pueblito*
> > > analyzing Emile Zola's *Germinal.*

Even though she writes "imprisoned," one gets a sense of relief in the last line, "analyzing Emile Zola's *Germinal.*" What work! Most farmworker children, and poor Chicano children, who make it to universities can make the immediate equation that writing a thesis is not equal to picking lettuce. It is good to sit, and read, and ponder, and write.

Mujer. Love, pain, grief, mourning for the lost. Frida. Gloria upholds Frida in the same way that Frida upholds us Chicanas, with passion, with drive, with honesty and sincerity, with the spirit of true Chicananess—we support and lean on each other—with great spirit. In "Frida and I" it is comforting to know that "Frida came today":

Frida came today,
I felt her close to me,
her thick braids and
her solitary stare,
following me,
reminding me that in blood
there is creation,
hope,
a new day
and that I like her
need to follow my destiny,
create,
dream...

Frida came today,
she sat next to me
and I cried on her shoulder...

And Frida embraced me,
she painted a new picture for me
filled with herself,
of her feminine strength...

The themes of love, loss of love(r), loneliness, solitude, existence and being, all of this exists in Gloria's poems. "But, are they good poems?" she asked when I talked with her. Somehow, I, a Chicana, never feel that I am in a position to respond (I ask the same of my own work.) but I can say that there is no other collection of poems by a Chicana that speaks like this to me.

These poems, like a brand new, shiny mirror, reflect parts of my past and who I am and who others are:

> My mother lives in these poems.
> My father lives in these poems.
> My sons and brothers live in these poems.
> The babies I did not have live in these poems.
> My daughter lives in these poems.
> I want my lover to see me in these poems.

Political poetry? Not really. The personal is always political. High art? My measuring stick says yes.

About Gloria Velásquez' poetry I say what Gloria says about Frida, "she exists and...will never abandon me to oblivion" ("Frida and I"); and about Gloria Velásquez' poetry I also say, "Gloria came today."

Margarita Luna Robles
Fresno, California

This book is dedicated to the memory
of my brother, John Robert Velásquez,
who died in Vietnam, May 6, 1968,

and

to my father, John E. Velásquez, who
died in Johnstown, Colorado on Veteran's Day, Nov. 11, 1992.

La pobreza

La pobreza duele
y llena todas mis venas.

Me hace recordar a un soldado
muriendo en un país extraño
y su familia sufriendo
por no tener dinero
para ir a verlo.

La pobreza destruye.
La pobreza se come lo bello
dejando aquello
que ese llama hambre—
hambre de sobrevivir.

Poverty

Poverty hurts
and it fills all of my veins.

It reminds me of a soldier
dying in a foreign country
and his family suffering
because they had no money
to go and search for him.

Poverty destroys.
Poverty devours all that is beautiful
leaving behind that
which is called hunger—
hunger for survival.

Recuerdos

De Johnstown, Colorado
    el desahije, los patrones,
    leña partida, agua fría.

De Alamosa, Colorado
    pizca de papas, colchones de paja,
    velas, aceite, cortinas de lona.

De Denver City, Tejas
    sudor, construcción,
    barrio de morenos, niños amontonados.

De Loveland, Colorado
    colonia aislada, escuelas blancas,
    lonches fríos, ropa usada.

De Greeley, Colorado
    college degree, automatic dishwasher,
    air conditioning, iced tea.

Memories

In Johnstown, Colorado
    thinning sugarbeets, the patrones
    chopped wood, ice-cold water.

In Alamosa, Colorado
    picking potatoes, straw mattresses
    candles, oil lamps, canvas curtains.

In Denver City, Texas
    sweat, construction workers,
    brown barrios, hoards of children.

In Loveland, Colorado
    segregated neighborhoods, white schools,
    cold lunches, used clothing.

In Greeley, Colorado
    college degree, automatic dishwasher,
    air conditioning, iced tea.

Bella juventud

Pregúntame qué aprendí en la escuela
ese tiempo feliz
de mi niñez y juventud,
en los fifties y los sixties.

Aprendí que Columbus
descubrió a América,
y que mis forefathers
fueron Washington y Roosevelt.

Aprendí que mi cultura
consistía en Dick y Jane,
con comidas americanas
de hot dogs y mustard.

Aprendí de prejudice
a los morenos y los spics,
porque los demás
con sus P.T.A. mothers
se olvidaron de nosotros.

Aprendí del sportsmanship
de anglo football players,
de anglo cheerleaders;
ignoraban a los morenos
que eran tontos y muy slow.

Aprendí de summer vacations,
swimming pools y suntans,
hincada en los files de betabel
con el azadón en las manos,
aguantando el calor.

Wonderful Youth

Ask me what I learned in school,
those joyful days
of my childhood and youth
in the Fifties and the Sixties.

I learned that Columbus
discovered América
and that my forefathers
were Washington and Roosevelt.

I learned that my "culture"
consisted of Dick and Jane
with American meals
of hot dogs and mustard.

I learned about prejudice
toward morenos and spics
because all the others
who had P.T.A. mothers,
forgot all about us.

I learned about sportsmanship
from Anglo football players,
from Anglo cheerleaders.
They avoided the greasers,
who were stupid and very slow.

I learned about summer vacations,
swimming pools and suntans,
stooped down in the beetfields
with a hoe in my hand
suffering the sun's heat.

¡Ay, qué bellos recuerdos
de ese tiempo feliz
de mi niñez y juventud,
en los fifties y los sixties.

Oh, what wonderful memories
of those joyful days
of my childhood and youth
in the Fifties and the Sixties.

Gente del sol

Gente del sol,
la tierra llora
por tus caricias
y
grita por sentir
la dulce firmeza
de tus manos empolladas.

Hija del sol,
la tierra goza de tu cuerpo
quemado y bronceado
y
sufre por tu ausencia
cuando al anochecer
te retiras bien cansada.

Hija del sol,
eres la inmortalidad
y siempre lo serás
y
cuando todo caiga,
por su debilidad
tú, hija del sol, vencerás.

Children of the Sun

Children of the Sun,
the earth laments
yearning for your caresses
          and
for the gentle firmness
of your dried-out
blistered hands.

Children of the Sun,
the earth pleasures in
your burned, bronzed body
          and
suffers from your absence
when you collapse exhausted
night after night.

Children of the Sun,
you're immortal now
and always will be
          and
when everything collapses
because of its frailty
you, child of the sun, will overcome.

Eres

Eres tan linda
con tus colores vivos,
rojo, blanco y azul.

Símbolo de la libertad.
Símbolo del americanismo.

Pero veo el ataúd
de un soldado,
una vez cubierto
de tus colores vivos.

Eras tan liviana,
tus colores vuelan dondequiera,
rojo, blanco y azul.

Símbolo de la democracia.
Símbolo de la humanidad.

Pero veo las lágrimas
de mi mamá
mientras te apretaba
y los balazos sonaban.

¡Eres tan linda!

Thou Art

You're so beautiful
in your bright colors,
red, white, and blue.

Symbol of freedom
Symbol of Americanism.

But I remember the coffin
of a young soldier
who was once covered
with your bright colors.

You're so light,
your colors fly in all directions,
red, white, and blue.

Symbol of democracy.
Symbol of humanity.

But I remember the tears
that my mother cried
as she held you tight
and the bullets rang out.

You're so beautiful!

Dalin

Me miraron ojos nublados
y dijo:
—I'm half man now, 'jita.
No good for nothing.

Enderezó su cuerpo marchito
y en una voz fuerte
ojos iluminados con su valor navajo
dijo:
—Ayer vino un hombre pa' enseñar
fotos de Nuevo México.
Llevaron a todos pa' verlos
y yo también fui.

—Este hombre dijo, "I've never seen
such dirty people as those Mexicans."
Este hombre era de aquí en Colorado.

—Yo me paré y le dije al hombre méndigo,
"I'm Mexican and don't be talking
that way 'bout my people."
Viejo méndigo, puerco. Le dije, "My
people were here before you."

Luego desapareció su valor nativo.
Entró su dolor de ser vivo
y dijo:
—Guess I stay here now, 'jita, till time comes.
No pude en el traila solo.
No puedo estar solo jamás.
Si estuviera tu nana...

Dalin

His storm-filled eyes looked at me
and he said,
"I'm half man now, 'jita.
No good for nothing."

He straightened out his bent body
and with a strong voice,
eyes illuminated by his Navajo pride,
he said,
"Yesterday, a man came t' show
some pictures of New Mexico.
They took everyone t' see them
and I went too."

"This man, he said, 'I've never seen
such dirty people as those Mexicans.'
This man, he was from here in Colorado."

"I stood up and I told the damned man,
'I'm Mexican and don't be talking
that way 'bout my people.'
That dirty pig. I told him, 'My
people were here before you.'"

Then his native pride disappeared,
replaced by his pain from still being alive
and he said,
"Guess I stay here now, 'jita, till time comes.
I couldn't make it in the trailer alone.
I can't be alone no more.
If only your Nana were here..."

—Bueno, 'jita. Ven cuando puedas.

Y sus ojos se ahogaban de lágrimas.

Fue entonces que recordé
al abuelito que me crió esos años de pobreza,
las canastas de comida del Salvation Army,
el dolor de la Nana y los hijos alcohólicos,
"la perra vida", como decía papá.

Y sí le pude contestar,
—Grandpa, I love you. I'll come again soon.

Pero todavía escondí las lágrimas.

"Okay, 'jita. Come when you can."

And his eyes were drowning in tears.

It was then that I remembered
the grandfather who raised me those poverty years,
the baskets of food from the Salvation Army,
Nana's pain and her alcoholic sons,
"the dog-life," as my father would say.

And, yes, I finally answered him,
"Grandpa, I love you. I'll come again soon."

But I still hid my tears.

¿Quién soy?

Soy Malinche,
mi cuerpo fue entregado a la esclavitud
y violado por el conquistador.

Soy la Virgen de Guadalupe,
mi imagen fue usada por padres opulentos
para convertir a mi pueblo indígena.

Soy la Llorona,
mi destino fue maldecido por aquellos
que me acusaron de matar a mis hijos.

Soy la Adelita,
mi presencia en las sangrientas frentes de batalla
fue ignorada por los hombres y la historia.

Soy la mujer indocumentada,
mi cuerpo está doblado por pizcar fresas
y por tallar los pisos de hoteles gringos.

¡Soy la Chicana revolucionaria,
mi voz grita por el Movimiento,
por los derechos humanos,
por mejores salarios y
por la igualdad social!

Who Am I?

I am Malinche,
my body was sold into slavery
and raped by the conquistador.

I am the Virgen de Guadalupe,
my image was used by opulent priests
to convert my indigenous race.

I am the Llorona,
my fate was damned by those who
accused me of murdering my own children.

I am the Adelita,
my presence on bloody battlefields
was ignored my men and history.

I am the undocumented woman,
my body is bent from picking strawberries
and scrubbing the floors in gringo hotels.

I am the revolutionary Chicana,
my voice cries out for El Movimiento,
for Human Rights,
for better wages and
for social equality!

Chicana

As I struggle to survive
in a world filled with
hardships,
disappointments,
and disillusionments,
I see the face of my nana,
and I feel her loving hands
caressing me
en las mañanas when
she made me my trencitas.

As I struggle through
roles I cannot endure,
woman,
Chicana,
mother, wife,
I see the gnarled, swollen
hands of my amá,
quietly making
her tortillas
tempranito en la mañana.

As I struggle to understand,
to seek answers to
fill the voids,
the needs
in my life,
I feel the strength of my mamá
cuando se iba al fil
y en la noche
volvía cansada
a más trabajo.

And from the images
of the strength of my raíces
I feel,
I am
Chicana,
And I will continue to survive.

Consejos

—¿Qué más quieres hija
si ya lo tienes todo?
Tu vida es perfecta
igual que tu marido.

—Pero mamá...

—Mira tu casita,
tan llena de recuerdos
¿Qué harás sin ella,
tan lejos de nosotros?

—Pero mamá...

—Y mira a tu niña,
tan llena de placer.
Por eso te pregunto,
¿Quién la va a mantener?

—Pero mamá...

—¿Y que dirá la gente
de una mujer que se va,
dejando a su marido
sin hacer caso a su mamá?

—Pero mamá...

—Las mujeres no van a la universidad.
No se necesitan educar.
Deben estar felices y
en su familia nomás pensar.

—Ay, mamá.

Advice

"What more do you want, hija?
You already have it all.
Your life is perfect
just like your husband."

"But, mamá."

"Look at your little house,
filled with so many memories.
What will yo do without it
so far away from us all?"

"But, mamá..."

"And look at your little girl
so happy and content.
That's why I'm asking you
Who's going to support her?"

"But, mamá..."

"And what will people say
about a woman who goes away
and leaves her husband
without listening to her mother?"

"But, mamá..."

"Women don't go to college.
They don't need an education.
They should be happy and
think only about their family."

"Ay, mamá."

Superwoman

Soy la Superwoman Chicana,
              planchando ropa,
              lavando platos,
              cuidando niños,
sin decir nada.

Soy la super-liberated Chicana
              asistiendo a clases,
              escribiendo ensayos,
              discutiendo la psicología,
sin decir nada.

Soy la super-macha Chicana
              arreglándote tu cafecito,
              trayéndote tu periódico,
              haciéndote tu comida.
sin decir nada.

Soy la super-pendeja Chicana
              bien, pero rebién
              cansada,
              oprimida y
              ahuitada.

Superwoman

I am the Superwoman Chicana,
   who irons clothes,
   washes dishes,
   takes care of children,
without saying a word.

I am the super-liberated Chicana
   who attends classes,
   writes essays,
   discusses psychology,
without saying a word.

I am the super-macha Chicana
   who prepares your coffee,
   brings your newspaper,
   cooks your meals,
without saying a word.

I am the super-pendeja Chicana,
   very, very tired,
   oppressed and
   fed up.

Un amante hindú

No aguanto la mediocridad,
las parejitas sentadas con sus hijos,
hartas y aburridas por su existencia.

No aguanto el silencio,
los mismos platos sucios de cada día,
el mismo piso sucio para barrer,
el mismo niño necio.

No aguanto los hombres
que no dicen nada interesante,
mediocres como los platos sucios
y los mismos huaraches viejos.

Quiero vivir con platos de cartón,
platos azules,
rectangulares,
con un amante hindú,
con niños diversos.

A Hindu Lover

I can't bear mediocrity,
docile couples sitting with their children,
fed up and bored by their existence.

I can't bear silence,
the same dirty plates everyday,
the same dirty floor waiting to be swept,
the same spoiled child.

I can't bear men
who have nothing interesting to say,
mediocrities like dirty plates
and the same old huaraches.

I want to live with paper plates,
blue plates,
rectangular plates,
with a Hindu lover,
with diverse children.

Déjenme morir

Quiero morir cuando haya amado
                    y sea amada
                              completamente,
                                        eternamente.

Quier morir cuando haya existido
                    y sea existente
                              simbólicamente,
                                        inmortalmente.

No quiero ser un reflejo
                    de un espejo.

No quiero ser una sombra
                    de una penumbra.

Y si esto me lo niegan
                    mientras me ahogan,
                              entonces,
                                        déjenme morir.

Then all of You, Let Me Die

I want to die after I've loved
                    and been loved
                              completely
                                        eternally.

I want to die after I've existed
                    and been existent
                              symbolically
                                        immortally.

I don't want to be a reflection
                    of a mirror.

I don't want to be a shadow
                    of a penumbra.

And if you deny me this
                    while suffocating me,
                              then, all of you,
                                        let me die.

If I Can Only Leave my Mark

Cuando muera,
    ¿seré otra losa gris de granito?

Pensará alguien en mí y dirá,
    "Sí, yo me acuerdo de ella. ¿Era la que manejaba el
    carro rojo?"
Pensará alguien en mí y dirá,
    "¿No era la que siempre andaba en su bicicleta?
    "¿No era la que vivía al otro lado de la calle?"

O pensará alguien en mí y dirá,
    "Sí, yo la conocía. La amaba tanto,
    Ella no está muerta—aún vive."

If I Can Only Leave My Mark

When I die, will I become just
    another gray slab of stone?

Will someone think of me and say,
    "Oh, I remember her. Didn't she drive a red car?"
Will someone think of me and say,
    "Wasn't she the one who always rode her bike?"
    "Didn't she live across the street?"

Or will someone think of me and say,
    "I knew her. I loved her,
    "She isn't gone—she still lives on."

Mi soledad

Nací en una soledad intensa
y moriré en una soledad inmensa.

Aunque penetres mi alma
nunca espantarás mi tristeza.

Me oirás hablar,
me oirás cantar,

Pero nunca jamás,
en mi soledad entrarás.

Porque nací en una soledad materna
y moriré en una soledad nocturna.

My Solitude

I was born in an intense solitude
and I will die in an immense solitude.

Even though you penetrate my soul
you'll never drive away my loneliness.

You will hear me speak,
you will hear me sing,

But never again
will you share in my solitude.

Because I was born in maternal solitude
and I will die in nocturnal solitude.

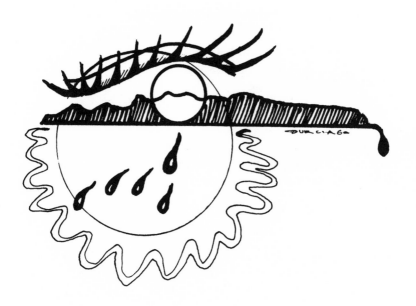

febrero

Tristes
estos momentos de mi vida,
sin salud,
sin bebé,
sin aquel hombre que me crió.

Y yo vagando sola en
un mar lleno de sangre,
de tumbas,
de caras oscuras.

Tristes,
estos momentos de mi vida.

February

Lonely
these moments in my life,
without my health,
without my baby,
without the man who nurtured me.

And I, navigating alone
in a sea of blood,
of tombs,
of shadowy faces.

Lonely,
these moments in my life.

Dimanche

hondo
pozo rectángulo
en el cementerio

vacío
botella aventada
del padre desilusionado

morado
moretones imprimidos
en los brazos de la madre

espeso
lágrimas de la muchacha
que se busca en el cristal

día eterno
como el aire
me doblas
y me sigues

Dimanche

deep
rectangular hole
in the cemetery

empty
discarded bottle
of a disillusioned father

purple
imprinted bruises
on a mother's arms

thick
a young girl's tears
as she searches in the mirror

eternal day,
like the wind,
you pass me by
and follow me

Mi amante

Tengo un amante que viene cada anoche.
Entra silencioso, jalándome a su lado
y me dejo llevar por suspiros de amor,
esas caricias tiernas de sus manos
que me amasan los senos.

Tengo un amante que siempre aparece,
me ama con fervor esas tristes noches
cuando ya no aguanto mis silencios,
los malditos recuerdos de Vietnam,
las palabras borrachas de papá.

Y mi amante se acuesta a mi lado,
me deja tocar sus caderas suaves,
aquel cuerpo tierno que me hace estremecer,
dándome esperanzas de un nuevo día,
de viajes nocturnos a su lado.

Tengo un amante que nadie puede ver
y no me abandona aunque llegue mi entierro.
Está nomás para la gloria.
Está solamente en mis versos.

My Lover

I have a lover who comes every night.
He arrives silent, pulling me to his side
and I'm swept away by murmurs of love,
those soft caresses of his hands
as they massage my breasts.

I have a lover who always appears,
he loves me with passion those lonely nights
when I can't bear my silences,
those damned memories of Vietnam,
dad's drunken words.

And my lover lays by my side.
He lets me touch his soft thighs,
that tender body that leaves me trembling,
giving me hope for a new day,
for nocturnal voyages at his side.

I have this lover that no one else can see,
who will never abandon me even upon my death.
He belongs only to gloria.
He's made only of my verses.

Despedida de Johnstown

Esa mañana
de calles dormidas,
no olí el perfume
de la fábrica de azúcar
ni el dulzor
del trigo amarillo
donde descalza jugaba
con los niños de la colonia;
no sentí las caricias
de caminos de tierra
donde me estacionaba
a besar a los novios;
no sentí los brazos
de fierro de mamá
ni el rostro hinchado
de papá,
los dos cicatrizados
por Vietnam;
no vi los files,
cuna de mi juventud
ni la casa
un álbum de recuerdos,
los retratos del Fini
la Primera Comunión y
aquellas paredes viejas
manchadas de sangre.

Hoy,
me paso los días
encerrada en esta ciudad fría
escuchando el tráfico,
leyendo cartas imaginarias,
viendo paredes de cemento,
respirando aire de aceite.

Farewell to Johnstown

That morning
of streets still asleep,
I didn't smell the perfume
from the town sugar factory
nor the sweetness
of the golden hayfields
where I played barefoot
with the children from the colony;
I didn't feel the caresses
of the dirt roads
where I once parked
with my boyfriends;
I didn't feel the iron embrace
of my mother's arms
nor my father's
swollen face,
both of them
scarred by Vietnam;
I didn't see the fields,
cradle of my youth
nor my parent's house
an album of memories,
Fini's pictures
our First Communion
and those old walls
stained with blood.

Today,
I spend my days
locked up in this cold city
listening to the traffic,
reading imaginary letters,
gazing at cement walls,
breathing the exhaust in the air.

Metamorfosis en Stanford

Ayer
escribía
versos
del alma,
gotas
frescas
cayendo,
derramándose
en calles,
en salas,
en páginas.

Ahora
me han
roto
el alma
en este
mundo
lleno de
teorías
inútiles,
palabras
burguesas,
y sólo
me queda
un aire
perdido
en la noche
que grita,
llora
por escapar.

Metamorphosis at Stanford

Yesterday
I wrote
verses
of the soul,
fresh
drops
falling,
spilling
on streets,
over classrooms,
on pages.

Now
they've
broken
my soul
in this
world
of useless
theories,
bourgeois
words,
and I'm
only left
with a lost
breeze
at night
that shouts,
cries out
for escape.

Realismo

allá,
    papá borracho
    mamá con pies hinchados
    abuelito rodando las calles

y yo aquí,
    encarcelada en Stanford
    lejos de mi pueblito
    analizando Germinal de Émile Zola.

Realism

Over there,
> my drunken father
> my mother with swollen feet
> my grandfather haunting the streets,

And me here,
> imprisoned at Stanford,
> far away from my pueblito
> analyzing Emile Zola's Germinal.

Autorretrato 1990

Soy la vieja mujer Navajo
Que te dio luz aquel día
detrás de un carromato
en la Tierra del Encanto.

Soy la vieja mujer Navajo
que meció a tu mamá
y le cantó rezos a los espíritus
en aquella reserva de Taos.

Soy la mujer joven Navajo
que se paró a tu lado
maldiciendo a los espíritus
la noche que moriste,
desheredado y olvidado
en aquella maldita casa de ancianos.

Soy el joven Navajo
que sueña con su tatarabuelo,
su espíritu bailando
en los picos de las montañas
en la Tierra del Encanto.

Abuelito,
Aubelito,
mi viejo tata indio

Yo jamás olvidaré.

Self-Portrait 1990

I am the old Navajo woman
who bore you that day
in a covered wagon
en la Tierra del Encanto.

I am the old Navajo woman
who rocked your mother to sleep
and chanted prayers to the spirits
in that old Taos Reservation.

I am the young Navajo woman
who stood by your side
cursing the spirits as you died
landless and forgotten
in that infernal rest home.

I am the young Navajo boy,
who dreams of his great-grandfather,
his spirit dancing on mountain peaks,
riding horseback at his side
en la Tierra del Encanto.

Grandfather,
Grandfather,
My old Indian Tata

I will not forget.

Frida y yo

Vino Frida hoy,
la sentí cerca de mí,
sus trenzas gruesas y
su mirada solitaria,
siguiéndome,
recordándome que en la sangre
hay creación,
esperanzas,
un nuevo día
y que yo como ella
debo seguir mi destino,
crear,
soñar,
amar a Esteban
como ella a Diego,
maldecir al hijo que no viene
como ella lo hizo día tras día.

Vino Frida hoy,
se sentó a mi lado
y lloré sobre su hombro.
Le conté de mis penas,
de la pluma seca,
de los ríos solitarios,
de aquel saber que existo
sin querer existir,
de aquel odiar a mi triste reflejo
día tras día,
de aquel saber morir
pedacito por pedacito.

Frida and I

Frida came today,
I felt her close to me,
her thick braids and
her solitary stare,
following me,
reminding me that in blood
there is creation,
hope,
a new day
and that I like her
need to follow my destiny,
create,
dream,
love Esteban
as she did Diego,
curse the unborn son
like she did day after day.

Frida came today,
she sat next to me
and I cried on her shoulder.
I told her of my pain,
of my dried pen,
of the solitary rivers,
of knowing that I exist
without wanting to exist,
of that hatred of my own reflection
day after day,
of knowing how to die
piece by piece.

Y Frida me abrazó,
me pintó un cuadro nuevo
lleno de ella
de su fuerza femenina,
de sus autorretratos perdidos,
de aquel amor eterno a Diego,
de aquel saber que existió
que existe
y que jamás me abandonará al olvido.

Vino Frida hoy.

And Frida embraced me,
she painted a new picture for me
filled with herself,
of her feminine strength,
of her forgotten self-portraits,
of that eternal love for Diego,
of knowing she existed,
that she exists
and that she will never abandon me to oblivion.

Frida came today.

Mi amante #2

Necesito un amante
que me detenga en los brazos
cuando me duele el alma y
mi cuerpo llora por libertad.

Necesito un amante
que me creará versos
de zapatos harapientos,
de sueños olvidados,
de bolsas de papel,
que entiende mi búsqueda
por la dignidad humana,
que llora por el niño abortado,
por el tata indio muriéndose de tristeza,
por los jóvenes muriéndose en guerras insensatas.

Necesito un amante verdadero,
no uno de versos vacíos,
ni de sueños románticos
sino de brazos, piernas y
un cuerpo para tenerme cerca.

My Lover #2

I need a lover
who will hold me close
when my soul aches and
my body cries out for freedom.

I need a lover
who for me will create verses
from old tattered shoes,
forgotten dreams
and brown paper bags,
who understands my
search for human dignity,
who cries for the aborted child,
for my Indian tata dying of loneliness,
for young men dying in senseless wars.

I need a real lover,
not one from empty verses,
nor romantic dreams
but one with arms, legs and
a body to hold me close.

Estos días de enero...

Sueño contigo en las noches
cuando me duele el alma
y las lágrimas caen,
cuando los libros me aburren
y volteo y volteo bajo las sábanas tibias
recordando aquel mar chino
donde tanto quise perderme,
irme lejos de su orilla,
para borrar las imágenes
Raúl rógandome aquel día en Chapultepec,
papá sangrando y sangrando
igual como Frida,
y tus ojos azules
que me han podido llevar lejos,
recordándome
cuánto he amado en la vida,
cuánto he perdido en estos días.

Sueño sin ti estos días de enero
caminando sola por los montes solitarios,
reconociendo bien que tú no me perteneces
y que yo jamás seré tuya,
y que otra vez,
este mar ingrato me ha engañado.

These Days in January...

I dream of you at night
when my soul is aching
and the teardrops fall,
when books bore me
and I toss and turn beneath
warm sheets,
remembering that wavy sea
where I wanted to lose myself,
run far away from its shore
to erase those images
Raúl begging me that day
in Chapultepec,
dad bleeding and bleeding
like Frida,
and your blue eyes
that have taken me far away,
reminding me
how much I have loved in my life,
how much I have lost these last days.

I dream without you these days in January
walking alone through solitary hills,
understanding altogether that you don't belong to me
and that I will never be yours,
and that once more,
that ungrateful sea has deceived me.

Black Birds

para Juan Kirk

Vinieron las bandadas de pájaros el día que moriste. Los oí llamándome. Oí sus alitas negras aleteando fuera de la ventana de mi recámara. Quería sacar la mano y tocarlos, detenerlos cerca, aliviar el anhelo que sentía dentro de mi matriz. Recordé a Frida entonces. Me imaginé dentro del yeso pesado, aquellas horas largas y tristes, el cuerpo pesado de Diego y los sangrientos fetos. Ay del útero vacío de Frida; ay del útero vacío mío.

Los oí cantando la noche que moriste. Traté de extenderme la mano, abrir la ventana para dejarlos entrar, pero las gotas pesadas de la lluvia seguían cayendo y yo supe que ya era muy tarde. Muy tarde para mi cuerpo adolorido y cansado. Muy tarde para todos esos cuerpitos jóvenes mutilados. Muy tarde para mis bandadas de pájaros negros cantando.

Los oí muriéndose esa noche. Oí sus gritos amortiguados cuando sus alitas se doblaron y cayeron, flotando en los charcos oscuros de agua sucia. Oí los gritos de Frida cuando el palo atravesó su cuerpo y yo sentí los fríos instrumentos de metal raspando mi alma.

Black Birds

for Juan Kirk

The flocks of birds came the day you died. I heard them calling me. I heard their black wings fluttering outside my bedroom window. I wanted to reach out and touch them, hold them close, sooth the yearning inside my womb. I remembered Frida then. I imagined myself inside the heavy plaster cast, those long, lonely hours, Diego's heavy body and the bleeding fetuses. Frida's empty womb, my empty womb.

I heard them singing the night you died. I tried to reach out, open up my window to let them come inside, but the rain came pouring down and I knew it was too late. Too late for my tired, aching body. Too late for all those young mutilated bodies. Too late for my flocks of singing black birds.

I heard them dying that night. I heard their muffled cries as their small wings folded and they fell, floating in the dark puddles of water. I heard Frida's screams as the wood pierced through her body and I felt the cold metal instruments scraping my soul.

Arturo

para Arturo Islas

Murió el Dios de la lluvia hoy,
dejándome sola para enfrentarme a mí misma
y a las memorias de aquellos años de Stanford.

"Es posible amar otra vez"?
te pregunté aquel día y
me contaste de Colette,
sus huaraches campesinos,
las brillantes y rojas uñas de pie,
el esposo que dejó depués de 13 años,
el amor que llamaba su favorita crudité,
diciéndome que a ella le hubiera gustado
mi "Fugitivo," los escritores Rasquachi
unidos en Zapata esa noche.
Y tú insististe en que te sentías cansado, no triste,
"Casi tengo 50 años," me bromeabas,
contándome de las Leyes de la Vida—
"Lo que das, por bien o por mal,
te lo devolverán mil veces."

Y ahora yo existo,
Suspiro.
Como.
Duermo.
Me la paso preguntándome quién estaría a tu lado
esa última noche triste de febrero.

¿Sería Colette?

Arturo

for Arturo Islas

The Rain God died today,
leaving me alone to face myself
and the memories of those Stanford years.

"Is it possible to love again?"
I asked you that day
and you told me about Colette,
her peasant sandals,
the bright, red painted toenails,
the husband she left after 13 years,
the love she called her "Favorite crudity,"
telling me that she would have liked
my "Fugitive," the Rasquachi writers
gathered at Zapata that night.
And you insisted you felt tired, not sad;
"Almost 50 years old," you joked,
telling me about Life's Laws—
"What you give, good and bad,
you get back a thousand-fold."

And now I exist.
I breathe.
I eat.
I sleep.
I go on wondering who was by your side
that last lonely night in February.

Was it Colette?

TASHUNKA WITCO

Crazy Horse vino a mi ventana hoy
y me murmuró palabras de fuerza y valor
mientras que yo lamentaba sueños no cumplidos,
deseando ser otra persona
en vez de esta poeta tonta.

"Allí está," me murmuró mi hijo esa mañana,
Y los dos nos quedamos mirando a Crazy Horse,
su pelo largo y grueso,
su perfil decidido,
decidido a liberar a su pueblo de esclavitud,
un sueño no cumplido como el mío.

Y luego Crazy Horse se fue,
montado en su caballo por las montañas de San Luis,
gritando palabras de libertad a los espíritus,
palabras que todavía resuenan en mi cabeza sentada aquí,
todavía una soñadora,
esperando su regreso.

TASHUNKA WITCO

Crazy Horse came to my window today
and whispered words of strength and courage
as I lay mourning dreams unfulfilled,
wishing I were someone else
instead of this foolish poeta.

"There he is," my young son whispered that morning.
And we both gazed at Crazy Horse,
the long thick mane of hair,
the dauntless profile,
determined to free his people from bondage,
a dream yet unfulfilled like my own.

And then Crazy Horse was gone,
riding off somewhere on the mountains of San Luis,
shouting words of freedom to the spirits,
words that still echo in my mind as I sit here,
a dreamer still,
waiting for his return.

B.I. Trevino '05

Zapatos negros

Sólo un par de zapatos negros,
zapatos de Vietnam,
tal vez de la marca 10,
tal vez los que usaste aquellas
noches que compartiste con el Louie,
fumando cigarros en la oscuridad
mientras las bombas caían
aquellas calientes noches tristes
recordando novias antiguas,
la noche que te robaste el carro de papá.

Sólo un par de zapatos negros,
zapatos de Vietnam,
tal vez de la marca 10,
tal vez los que usabas
cuando lavabas tu ropa
o caminabas al refugio del Louie
para compartir las tortillas y el chile
que acababa de mandarte mamá,
aquellas oscuras noches tristes
recordando la colonia vieja,
los carros requiados de mi tío Arturo.

Sólo un par de zapatos negros,
zapatos de Vietnam,
los zapatos del Fini
manchados de sangre,
la peste de la guerra,
los gritos penetrantes de mamá,
los ojos alcohólicos de papá,
el corazón partido del Louie
y mi alma herida
mientras me fijo día tras día

Black Shoes

Just another pair of black shoes,
Vietnam shoes,
maybe a size 10,
maybe the ones you wore
the nights you shared with Louie,
smoking cigarettes in the dark
while the bombs exploded,
those hot lonely nights
remembering old girlfriends,
the night you stole Dad's car.

Just another pair of black shoes,
Vietnam shoes,
maybe a size 10,
maybe the ones you wore
when you washed your clothes
or walked to Louie's bunker
to share the tortillas and chile
mom had just sent,
those dark, lonely nights
remembering the old colonia,
Uncle Arthur's junked cars.

Just another pair of black shoes,
Vietnam shoes,
Fini's shoes
stained with blood,
the stench of war,
mom's piercing cries,
dad's alcoholic eyes,
Louie's broken heart
and my wounded soul
as I stare day after day

en esos viejos zapatos negros
abandonados en mi ropero,
esperando,
anhelando tu regreso.

at those old, black shoes
sitting in my closet,
waiting,
hoping for your return.

De Good Morning, Vietnam
a Good Morning, Mamá

¿Te acordaste de él hoy, mamá? ¿de aquel niño que cargaste en tu vientre aquellos días de invierno cuando no sabías ni de dónde vendría el pan de ese día, de esos tiempos de pobreza, de casas prestadas, patrones fríos y un cuarto frío donde nació aquel niño que tú adoraste hasta el día en que te lo quitaron para siempre?

¿Te acordaste de él hoy, mamá? ¿Pensaste en aquella noche cuando lo pariste en aquel cuarto oscuro, sin saber de dónde vendría el dinero para pagar al doctor, de aquel joven esposo que no sabía cómo mantener a una mujer y un niño sin perderse en la borrachera con sus amigos, dejándote sola con remordimientos.

¿Te acordaste de él este día de su cumpleaños, mamá, este 27 de enero mientras tallabas los pisos de los baños de los turistas, mientras les preparabas sus lonches a los viejitos, mientras esculcabas la cara de tu marido para ver si el maldito alcohol lo habría poseído?

Yo sí pensé en él, mamá. Yo sí pensé en aquel muchacho de pelo negro y rizado que se acostaba a mi lado, que jugaba a las canicas conmigo en la tierra en las casas de los patrones, de aquel adolescente que fumaba cigarros a la escondida y me rogaba que no te lo dijera.

Yo sí pensé en él, mamá, pensé en sus facciones, en su cara güera, en su camiseta blanca, en el olor de su piel quemada y sus gritos mientras rodaba en la maldita arena gritando, "Mamá, ¿dónde estás? ¡papá!" y la peste de la guerra, los muertos, las ametralladoras y un cajón cerrado para siempre.

Sí, mamá, hoy pensé en él, hoy me morí un poco más al recordar las últimas palabras que me dijo, "Adiós, fea. Escríbeme pronto."

From Good Morning, Vietnam to "Good Morning, Mom."

Did you remember him today, mom, that child you carried in your womb those winter days when you didn't even know where the next day's meal was coming from, those days of poverty, of borrowed houses, cold-hearted patrones and a small cold room where the son you adored was born?

Did you remember him today, mom? Did you think about that night when you bore him in that small dark room without having any idea where the money would come from to pay the doctor, that young husband who didn't know how to support a woman and a child without losing himself in drunkenness with his friends, leaving you all alone and filled with bitterness.

Did you remember him on his birthday, mom, this 27th day of January, while you scrubbed the tourists' bathroom floors, while you prepared lunch for your elderly people, while you searched your husband's face to see if that damned alcohol had already possessed him?

I did think about him today, mom. I did think about that young boy with black wavy hair who slept by my side, who played marbles with me in the dirt in the borrowed houses of the patrón, that young adolescent who used to hide and smoke cigarettes, begging me not to tell on him.

I did think about him, mom; I thought about his features, his light-skinned face, his white T-shirt, the smell of his burnt skin and his screams as he rolled in the damned sand shouting, "Mom, where are you? Dad!" And the stench of war, the dead bodies, the machine guns, and a coffin closed forever.

Yes, mom. I thought about him today. Today I died a little more as I remembered the last words he said to me, "Goodbye, fea. Write to me soon."

Carta a un patroncito

Patroncito,

No puedo deshacerme de ti. Parece que andas por todas partes. Me acuerdo cuando el Fini y yo teníamos cinco años y vivíamos en tu rancho, esas botas de vaquero, tu blanca cara arrogante gritándoles órdenes a mis padres. Y cuando tenía diez años, me acuerdo de la misma cara blanca dándonos más órdenes. Todavía puedo escuchar al Fini arreglando tu jardín mientras que mamá y yo limpiábamos tu casa grande. Años después, nos fuimos de tu choza para siempre y al llegar a mis años de adolescente, tu misma cara lasciva aparecía en cada esquina de la calle, en el viejo molino donde papá trabajaba, en la fábrica de azúcar, en los files de betabel donde trabajaba en el verano con mi Apá.

Patroncito,

Yo crecí y me fui, dejándote detrás para que destruyeras a mi mamá aquel día que le dijiste que mi papá era un canalla. Huí de ti, eso creía, a Califas, a un mundo académico donde pensaba que no me podrías encontrar, así lo creía. Y luego un día, allí estabas otra vez, tu sonriente cara blanca en la Cámara de Educación Pública en San Luis Obispo tratando de destruir el orgullo de una Chicanita, diciéndole que ella no valía nada. Pero yo me enfrenté contigo esta vez, no me dejé vencer por tu cancerosa cara sonriente. Y ganamos; dejaron que regresara mi Chicanita a la escuela y tú desapareciste, así lo pensaba, hasta ayer cuando volteé una esquina y allí estabas otra vez, siguiéndome, molestándome, tratando de destruir mi orgullo como lo hiciste con el de mi mamá. Y lloré otra vez. Lloro cada día de miedo porque sé que tú estás oculto detrás de las esquinas esperando que yo pase.

Patroncito,

¿Por qué no me dejas sola? ¿No ves el fuerte orgullo de mi sangre návajo y el de mis antepasados? Corre libre como el viento sobre las cimas de las montañas, bailando suave con el espíritu del Dalin. Patroncito, ¿por qué tienes que conquistar y destruir como lo hiciste con todos los que vinieron antes?

Letter to a Patroncito

Patroncito,

I can't seem to get away from you. You seem to be everywhere my tired feet take me. I remember when Fini and I were five years old living on your farm, those cowboy boots, that white smiling face shouting orders to my parents. And when I turned ten, I remember the same white face still ordering us around. I can still hear Fini mowing your lawn while mom and I cleaned your big house. Years later, we left your run-down shack for good and as I grew into my teenage years, your leering face appeared in every street corner, at the old hay mill where dad worked, at the sugar factory, in the beetfields where I worked in the summers with apá.

Patroncito,

I moved away from my pueblito. I left you behind to destroy my mother that day you told her that my father was no good, to just let him bleed to death. I ran away from you, I thought, to Califas, to an educated world where you couldn't find me, I thought. And then one day, there you were again, your white smiling face on the San Luis Obispo school board destroying a young Chicanita's self-respect, telling her she wasn't any good. But I stood up to you; I didn't give in to your cancerous smiling face. And we won; my Chicanita went back to school and you disappeared, so I thought, until yesterday when I turned a corner and there you were again, following me, hounding me, attempting to destroy my self-respect and that of my people as you did my mother's. And I cried again. I cry everyday now in fear because I know you're there lurking behind corners just waiting for me.

Patroncito,

Why can't you leave me alone? See my strong, proud Navajo blood and that of my ancestors? It runs free like the wind on the mountaintops, dancing gently with Dalin's spirit. Patroncito, why can't you go away? Why must you conquer and destroy all those who came before you?

Despedida de Juan

Vinieron a despedirse de su rey que se moría
ese día triste de noviembre.
Sentada a su lado,
me quedé mirándolos a todos,
recordando las palabras del doctor todos esos años:
"El ya no sirve para la sociedad, está sólo agotando Medicare.
Llévenselo a la casa a morir."

Y tuve visiones de aquel padre tierno
que había conocido toda mi vida,
el hombre humilde nacido en 1931
en una casita prestada en las afueras del pueblo,
el joven muchacho que dejó la escuela
para trabajar en el campo,
enterrando para siempre sus sueños y dejando
su orgullo atrás en botellas vacías de cerveza.

Lo llevamos a la casa para morir ese día,
ayudándole al hombre débil y amarillo a subirse
de la silla de ruedas a la camioneta de mi primo Arturito,
dejando para siempre aquel hospital que odiaba,
dirigiéndose a su casa de los últimos veinticuatro años,
el descolorido sillón café,
la recámara llena de libros de bolsillo,
viejas novelas de vaquero,
los anillos que le encantaba llevar,
el retrato de su único hijo en la pared
de la casa que el gobierno le dio
a cambio de una vida,
la esposa que adoró todos esos años de pobreza,
pizcando algodón en Tejas, desahijando betabel,
viviendo en chozas desvencijadas del patrón

Farewell to Juan

They came to say goodbye to their dying king,
on that sad November day.
Sitting at his side,
I watched them all,
remembering the doctor's advice all those years:
"He's no good to society, just using up Medicare.
Take him home to die."

And I had visions of the gentle father
I had known all my life,
the humble man born in 1931 in a farm laborer's shack
on the outskirts of town,
the young boy who left school to work in the fields,
forever burying his dreams and leaving
his pride behind in empty beer bottles.

We took him home to die that day,
helping the weak, jaundiced man climb
from the wheelchair into Arturito's van,
leaving the hospital he hated,
heading for his home of twenty-four years,
the faded brown armchair,
the bedroom filled with paperbacks,
old westerns, the rings he loved to wear,
the picture of his only son hanging on the wall
of the house the government gave him
in exchange for a life,
the wife he adored all those years of poverty,
picking cotton, hoeing sugarbeets,
living in run-down farmer's shacks

con la joven de diecinueve años que le dio dos hijos,
la hija por medio de la cual vivió,
la del doctorado que adoraba
al hombre callado que abandonó la escuela en el séptimo grado
el hombre que se negó a morir en una cama del hospital,
rogándole, "Llévenme a la casa."

Y vinieron las bandadas de gente ese Día de Veteranos,
sus ahijados, el padre Steve, su compadre Nacho,
mi tío Arturo con todos sus hijos,
siguieron viniendo en bandadas
como mis mirlos trayendo regalos,
una docena de huevos de su compadre Jesús,
tamales de su comadre Quica,
caras de mi pasado lejano,
contándome historias de cómo mi papá les había ayudado:
"Me acuerdo del día que no teníamos leña ni carbón,
tu papá nos cortó llantas viejas para calentar la casa.
Le debemos mucho a mi compadre."

Y lo enterramos en una tumba del cementerio
donde su único hijo lo esperaba,
cerca del lugar donde había nacido
en el pueblito de Colorado que tanto amó.

Sí, yo me acuerdo de papá,
el padre del Fini que,
finalmente, a su hijo encontró.

with the nineteen year old girl
who bore his two children,
the daughter he lived through,
the one with the Ph.D. who worshipped
the quiet man with the 7th grade education,
the man who refused to die in a hospital bed,
begging her, "Llévenme a la casa."

And the flocks of people came that Veteran's Day,
his ahijados, Father Steve, his compadre Nacho,
my tío Arturo with his sons and daughters.
They kept coming in flocks
like my black birds,
bearing gifts,
a dozen eggs from his comadre Quica,
faces from my distant past,
telling me stories of how my father helped them:
"I remember the day we had no wood or coal, your
daddy cut up old tires for us to heat the house.
We owe my compadre a lot."

And so we buried him in the cemetery plot
where his only son lay waiting,
next to the place where he was born in
the small Colorado town he once loved.

Yes, I remember Dad,
Fini's dad,
who finally found his son.

Días ya pasados en Orange County

Añoro esos días ya pasados,
la delgada muchacha que antes fui,
vestida de collares de cuentas,
el barbudo Chicano a mi lado,
gritando palabrotas a las multitudes,
agitando pancartas de paz,
tomando cerveza en cantinas callejeras
con el Cowboy y sus perros,
los Beatles
y el olor de rancio moscatel.

Añoro esos días ya pasados,
Martin Luther King Jr.,
"Nigger lovers," nos gritaban,
colas de asistencia social y bonos para comer,
Vietnam chorreando de todos los agujeros,
el olor de la piel quemada del Fini,
el ataúd cerrado
y los gritos de mamá.

Maldigo esos días ya pasados
sentada aquí en mi oficina
rodeada de la mediocridad,
alcahuetes académicos,
Martin Luther King Jr. muerto en la pared,
las cartas de Vietnam arregladas nítidamente en el estante,
el moscatel rancio ya agotado,
el barbudo Chicano ya ido,
los buenos viejos días ya pasados.

Days Gone by in Orange County

I mourn for those days gone by,
the slim-waisted girl I once was,
dressed in beads,
the bearded Chicano at my side,
screaming obscenities at the crowds,
waving peace signs,
drinking beer in honky-tonk bars
with Cowboy and his dogs,
the Beatles
and the smell of stale muscatel.

I mourn for those days gone by,
Martin Luther King Jr.,
"Nigger lovers," they shouted at us,
welfare lines and food stamps,
Vietnam pouring out of the cracks,
the smell of Fini's burnt skin,
the closed coffin
and my mother's screams.

I curse those days gone by
sitting here in my office
surrounded by mediocrity,
academic pimps,
Martin Luther King Jr. dead on the wall,
letters from Vietnam neatly stacked on the shelf,
no more stale muscatel,
no more bearded Chicano,
no more days gone by.

Autorretrato 1991

Soy una escritora Chicana.
¿Moriré en la obscuridad?
¿Quedarán mis versos enterrados
en viejas cajas polvorientas?
Olvidados.
Abandonados.

Soy una escritora Chicana.
Escribo de la guerra y de
mis jóvenes soldados morenos
de la muerte constante de mi pueblo
en comunidades obscuras,
víctimas como yo.
Olvidados.
Abandonados.

Soy una escritora Chicana.
¿Se acordarán mis hijos de mí
¿Murmurarán los Dioses mi nombre?
¿Anhelará la sociedad mis palabras tristes?
¿O seré enterrada al lado de aquellas
otras voces silenciadas?

Soy una escritora Chicana.
Me nego a ser callada,
a ser enterrada en la obscuridad.
Olvidada.
Abandonada.

Self-Portrait 1991

I am a Chicana writer.
Will I die in obscurity?
Will my verses remain buried
in dusty, old boxes?
Forgotten.
Abandoned.

I am a Chicana writer.
I write about war and
my young brown soldiers,
about the constant death of my people
in obscure communities,
victims like me.
Forgotten.
Abandoned.

I am a Chicana writer.
Will my children remember me?
Will the Gods whisper my name?
Will society yearn for my lonely words?
Or will I be buried alongside
those other silenced voices?

I am a Chicana writer.
I refuse to be silent,
to be buried in obscurity.
Forgotten,
Abandoned.

Edúcate

Edúcate, Raza,
young Chicanitas
women warriors of Aztlán.

Hey, homeboy,
I'm not ready to have babies,
smoke dope or die
from gang wars in the barrio.

I want to spread my wings,
soar high above the skies,
get a Ph.D.,
become a scientist,
teach our children in
the barrios of Aztlán.

Edúcate, Raza,
young Chicanitas
women warriors of Aztlán.

Hey, homegirl,
I don't want to hang out
get pregnant
or be a drop out.

I want to be somebody,
write verses,
create dreams
be a leader like Dolores Huerta.

Edúcate, m'ija,
me decía mi mamá,
me decían mis tías,
their faces tired,
their bodies bent from
picking strawberries,
scrubbing floors in hotels.

Edúcate mujer,
Adelante mujer,
the future is yours.

América

"Oh beautiful
for spacious skies
for amber waves of grain.
For purple mountain's majesty
above the fruited plain..."
América
América
you bring me shame today
with your star-spangled
red white y blue
and your racist policies
y políticos.

Quoting
L. A. Times, March 21, 1996,
The House passed an ammendment
to the immigration-reform bill that
allows states to deny public education
to children who are in this country illegally.
And Pete Wilson said,
"This is a hard-earned victory for the people
of California who have made it clear time and
 time again that they do not want to foot the bill
 for continued illegal immigration."

And Newt Gingrich said,
"There is no question that offering free
taxpayer goods to illegals attracts more illegals...,"
"It is wrong to be the welfare capital of the world."

And I say
Chale, ése.
This is Aztlán
where my people were born.
My ancestors didn't come on ships
across the ocean blue.
Their roots are embedded en la tierra
y en el nopal
in this imaginary line that you invented
to repress and oppress.

"Oh, say can you see
by the dawn's early light
what so proudly we hailed
at the twilight's last gleaming..."

Quoting L. A. Times, April 2, 1996
In dramatic videotape aired repeatedly
on local television, Riverside County
sheriff's deputies on Monday violently
clubbed two suspected illegal immigrants
in South El Monte after a high speed chase...
And Dan Swift, president of the Riverside
County Sheriff's Association said, "We are
100% behind our deputies. The department
is expected to investigate allegations of force,
but so far the facts aren't in. All we have are 15
seconds of videotape and a whole lot of excitement."

And Riverside County assistant District Attorney,
Randy Tamagi insisted that the taped clubbing,
"is not a racial issue. It is an incident that arose
from a stressful situation."

América
América
You bring me shame today.
Y coraje
As I take to the streets
protestando otra vez
My banner held high
Chicano Movement revived
César a mi lado,
shouting "Down with 187!
We didn't cross no borders.
They crossed us."

"My country 'tis of thee
sweet land of liberty
of thee I sing.
Land where my fathers died.
Land of the pilgrim's pride.
From every mountainside
Let freedom ring."

About The Author

Gloria Velásquez is an award winning writer of poetry and fiction who graduated from Stanford University in 1985 with a Ph.D. in Latin American & Chicano Literatures. Her poetry and short stories have been published in numerous journals and anthologies such as: *From the Midwest to the West* (Chicano-Riqueño Studies Publication, 1980); *Southwest Tales* (Maize Press, 1986); *Palabra Nueva Cuentos Chicanos II* (Dos Pasos Editores, 1986); *Chicanos y Chicanas en Diálogo* (Quarry West Magazine, 1989); *Best New Chicano Literature* (Bilingual Review Press, 1989);and *Neueste Chicano Lyrik* (Bamberg, Germany, 1994). *Chicano Literature: 1965 - 1995* (Garland Press, 1997)Velásquez is the author of the Roosevelt High School Book Series for young adults which features teenagers of different ethnicities: *Juanita Fights the School Board, Maya's Divided World,* and *Tommy Stands Alone.*

One of Chicano Literature's most distinguished authors, Gloria Velásquez was selected for inclusion in *Who's Who Among Hispanic Americans,* 1994-1995, and in *Chicano Writers: Second Series,* Dictionary of Literary Biography, edited by Francisco Lomelí and Carl Shirley. Velásquez also received the 11th Chicano Literary Prize in the Short Story from the University of California at Irvine, 1985. At Stanford University, she was awarded the Premier and Deuxième Prix in poetry (1979) from the Department of French & Italian. In 1989, Velásquez became the first Chicana to be inducted into the University of Northern Colorado's Hall of Fame for her achievements in creative writing.

Gloria Velásquez is currently a Professor in the Modern Languages and Literatures Department at California Polytechnic State University in San Luis Obispo, California, where she resides with her family.

About the Cover Artist

G. Bermúdez is a self-taught Chicano artist originally from Southern California who has received several awards for his art-work. Of special significance, he is the creator of the original "Superwoman Chicana" artwork (based on Gloria Velásquez's poem, "Superwoman") which was used for Velásquez's "Superwoman T-shirt design and greeting card (available through Serpiente Emplumada). Another of Bermúdez's important art pieces, "America," which protests California's Proposition 187, was recently published on a post card. G. Bermúdez is currently work-ing on illustrations for upcoming novels by Gloria Velásquez.

About the Illustration Artists

José Antonio Burciaga, one of Chicano literature's most beloved authors, who recently passed away, was born in El Paso and taught at Stanford University. His book *Undocumented Love* won the Before Columbus American Book Award for poetry. His other books include *Drink Cultura: Chicanismo* and *Spilling The Beans: Lotería Chicana.* He was a winner of the Hispanic Heritage Award for Literature.

Brandi Treviño, the author's daughter, is a Chicana artist from Colorado. She has received several awards for her artwork. Most recently, her artwork was used in the 1992 Koger Kamp Foundations posters and T-shirts. She is currently a student at the University of Colorado in Boulder, Colorado.

Robert John Velásquez Treviño (a native of California) is an eighth grade student at Old Mission School. He lives in San Luis Obispo with his mother, the author. His artwork has been on exhibit at the Multi-Cultural Center at Cal Poly, San Luis Obispo, California. He has also won several awards in both poetry and prose.